1

The Song That I Sing

Poetry with the rhythm of life

by D. Skowera

2

to my mother and father

ISBN 978-0-578-01338-1

3

Contents

Black And White

I keep them black and white.
I keep them still in time.
Their smiles never fade.
Their feet never tire.
This glass is strong.

I keep them in wood-
I keep it black.
I keep them all the same.
Their joy is well-protected.
Their moment is forever.

I keep them all together.
I keep them as close as I can.
I keep them high on the white wall.
Their feet will never dirty.
Their pain will never reach them.

I say my prayers in black and white
And hang them on the wall.
I keep them close to heaven.
I keep them close to me.
I keep them as I remember them.
I keep them as they should be.

Amazing Grace

Amazing grace,
How sweet the sound,
That saved its best for me.

I paid the cost,
Until I drown.
Now, I'm broke,
But finally free.

Remember Them

He has no first name
And never gets to see
His supposed atrocities
Broadcast on t.v.

He has no first name
And can't remember the feel
Of blue jeans or a woman's skin
Only BDUs and steel

She has no first name
And I don't think she'd care
What the new trend is this month
Or what you think of her hair

He has no bed of his own
And I bet he'd love a beer
Or to see how much his son has grown
And changed within a year

She has no shoes to dance in
No dress to twirl around
No child to bounce upon her knee
Only boots to hit the ground

Remember them in front of the college
Or when you watch the morning news
While you drink coffee that tastes like coffee
And debate each other's views

Remember them when you go home
And you can't even tell
Just how much your son has grown
Because you know him so well

Remember them even though
You just may never see
How much freedom that they have given
To someone's sons across the sea

The Road Without Me

You're on a road without me-
  In a car with an empty seat.
You're sleeping in a bed
  Too big for just two feet.

Your arms must feel empty
  Without me there to hold.
Are you missing any pieces,
  Of the stories that I've told?

When you hear my name spoken,
  Does it make you think of me?
Or is it just a word,
  Passing through the scenery?

The girl with long, brown hair-
  Does she make you second-look?
Is there a gape upon your shelf,
  Where there's that nagging, missing book?

Do you hear a song playing,
  That brings back a memory?
Do the words mean something different,
  When you think of me?

The Road Without You

I'm on a road without you,
  In a bed that's much too small;
Have your number and a phone,
  But I just can't make the call.

Every decent man I meet
  Seems to, also, have your name.
Every smile that they give me
  Just can't make me feel the same.

The thousand things I'm learning,
  And the beauties that I see,
Seldom bring me enjoyment
  Because you're not here with me.

Keep your picture on the wall,
  So that I'll never forget
What the face of love looked like,
  And the remnants of its debt.

I'm on a road without you,
  In a world without you near.
I swear I just don't exist;
  It's no life without you here.

Iron Man

You raised this child in reverse,
With stone heart, but loving verse.

With iron fist and hurtful prank,
I couldn't swim, but never sank.

You made a man out of a little girl,
But gave each color you had in the world.

When first I saw you cry, I knew:
That even iron men melt too.

And your little man's a woman now;
Her iron man has a fading brow.

But it's the iron man that I have to thank,
When each stone that hits me, crumbles to the bank.

For these bones of mine-they came from *you;*
Which means that I'm half iron too.

So, Dad, you can rest easy now,
Even though, your little man's a girl.
Nothing in life will ever hurt her,
Because *you* brought her into this world.

I'm Still Here

Alone, there stands the Iron Man,
Who gazes out across the land,
That caused each line in calloused hand.

He stands atop all that remains:
Of what he built and weathered grains,
All paid with loving, labored pains.

A twisted pole hangs down to sigh,
Where, again, he raised the flag to fly.
Surviving, together, they defy.

From crumbled stairs is not a tear.
From weathered flag there is no fear.
They stare in silence, *I'm still here.*

My father, after surviving a tornado that destroyed our home.

The Song That I Sing

There is a road that can't be traveled.
There is a dream in a dream.
I walk along the clock alone
And you are the song that I sing.
There are words in the air,
Which pass from you and I,
On the road that can't be traveled-
In this song that knows no time.
No one hears this symphony
Resounding in my heart.
These colors are not visible
Which permeate my heart.
I walk along the clock alone
And hear only one thing:
My voice traveling a road I can't,
For you-
The song that I sing.

What You've Done To Beauty

I refuse to be beautiful.

My hair was once soft
And glistened in the sunlight
Whispering a hint of auburn
From my mother

This skin was felt dew
No matter how much I weathered it
In the sun of the fields

My heart never knew
Sarcasm
Or self-defense

These hands were once scarless
These hands never knew how to make fists

I never knew I was beautiful

Now, I only know *then*
And refusing to be beautiful

Beauty is a ticket into a dark alley for a young girl

She either never makes it out of the alley
Or emerges
A different creature
Manipulative and cold
Yearning to keep that glistening and felt dew for her survival

I fought through the side of a shadow

Who is she?
We couldn't have taken her down the alley?
But wait...
Her hair almost glistens...

Or does it?
And her skin...
Could it be felt dew?
No.
Maybe not.

I wear my ugliness like a jewel
Anything that doesn't match
Matches me

I wrap my locks so tight
A thousand suns couldn't make them glisten

You don't know me
I'm not *her*

I refuse to be beautiful
After what you've done to beauty.

13

A Prayer for the Widow

God, please comfort his soul,
For she cannot help but cry.
I pray that he can't hear,
The sorrow of his Goodbye.

Please don't let the dead know,
All the pain they've left behind;
We don't mean to haunt them,
There's just too much to remind.

Lord, please don't let him hear-
How she sometimes falls apart,
Although she cannot help it.
I know it would break his heart.

*for my sister after the loss of her husband

14

Someday

Someday I hope to see you
Coming towards me down the street
With the arms and smile I've dreamt about
And the love I've longed to meet

Someday I hope to see you
And stop as I pass you by
At the sound of a laughter I once knew
Before we last said goodbye

Someday I hope to see you
Standing with me by my side
To share in the beauties that I find
Building memories by the tide

Someday I hope to see you
Coming towards me down the street
But laugh at thoughtful resemblances
That comfort me till we meet

*I sat in a café, 2,000 miles away from home and thought I saw my father walking down the street. How the mind will play tricks on us.

The Nuts and Bolts of it All

Sleep is just another word
  For trying to close your eyes.

Love is just another man
  Who's found himself a disguise.

Keeping faith in God is swell,
  If you've got a dime to spare,

And doubting that you'll go to Hell
  Will surely get you there.

Pain is just another word,
  For an awareness of Life.

Being good at "being good"
  Won't help you find a wife.

*what I thought I'd learned by the age of 19.

We Two

We two-
Born of a different wind;
Will deny the turbulence,
Until it feels as if we've sinned.

We two-
Born of a different time,
Will curse our eyes for feeling,
Although they've done no crime.

We two-
Born of a similar song,
Will drown in our self-resistance,
Until the pain is gone.

Reckoning

You are my house, I have no home.
You hear a voice that does not speak.
You found my booming echoes
      in the canyons of my soul.
How long I've thought this treasure
      would sleep a thousand years,
      until the dust had turned to dust
      and abandoned thoughts just disappear.
The wandering around about
      of a subconscience inside-out
      was such a wound to show the sun,
      was such a feast to dine alone.
My smile weeps with bafflement-
      has ignorance met content?
What is the cost of reckoning
      and to view the soul's equivalent?

Dancing

Tell me something beautiful
Let it get under my skin
Make it chase the fear away
That I've been living in

Love was meant to be
A floor we twirl about
My shoes are around here somewhere
I just never bring them out

Did I stumble on myself
Or step on too many feet
Have I never loved a song
Or can I just not keep the beat

I'm scared as hell and you are too
But come ask me for a dance
Just pick me out a slow one
While I'm willing to take a chance

Traces Of You

I often wish that you would go.
  There's no humor in your haunting.
  There's no release after your flaunting.
And a dream is difficult to lie next to.

I wish that when I turn around,
  I don't see something that you cared for.
  It seems I'm always in store
For a trace of you to be found.

I may deserve what I got,
  But I wish that I was free,
  Because even though you left me
There's a few things you forgot.

A Thing That Can't Be Named

Who cages a human being

in a small barbed wire cage?

Who kidnaps a total stranger

because a government caused them rage?

Who cuts a father's head off

for all the world to see?

Who rapes a politician

to produce a guerrilla baby?

Who proudly totes a weapon

to boast a title with the word "terror"?

Who threatens to kill

those that say a different prayer?

Who are the fools that confused

revered with being feared?

Who are these self proclaimed bullies that were no contest

for legislation and citizens that voted for the best?

Who are these men and women

that pout like an unschooled child,

and let their own grow up in violence,

like a thing among the wild?

Who uses poetry

to promote recruitment?

Who thinks that rhyming ugliness

will beautify intent?

Who are these cowards that can't accept the fact

the world deserves different freedoms,

they have no right to take back?

Who thinks because they can end a life

that they had the right to take it?

Who thinks disagreeing with a law

means that they can break it?

What is this thing that calls itself a man?

Who is this mother that would rather kill?

What is this child with a predestined plan?

Who thinks they deserve to bend our will?

Written after working on a case of rescued hostages. It was not my job to make sense of it, but I found myself asking these questions that night.

Wasted Talent

It is a wicked cruelty-
The kind of power given to fire.

We flock,
Unquestioning in our blindness,
To feel the nurture of a warmth we cannot resist.

It is a wicked cruelty-
This beaconing ability
That consumes the trusting.

I never want to fall in love.

My Super Power Request

I want to soak the world with love songs
The kind that absorb an empty room
And force the most reserved kind
To sing into a broom
I want to possess the power of that gift
The embrace of a melody
That can turn a horrid day into new found hopeful bliss
The feeling of a kiss without the kiss
I want to write a love song
That makes the lonely not alone
I want to make a sound resound
Long after the sound has gone
I wish that I could write love songs
So the fools can still be fools
And the wooers have fuel
To continue breaking rules
Until the fools finally get wise
I wish I was a love song
But they don't make them in my size

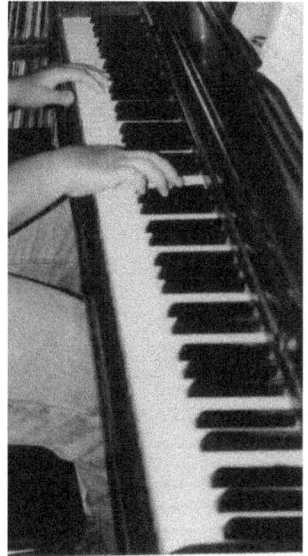

Until Were You

I was, so long, a stone
Never skipping, all alone
You stirred a current in my heart
And brought a wind of change
The ocean never was
Until were you
You taught my mind
Of possibility redefined
Now I stagger on the fear
Of holding something near
But the ocean never was
Until were you
I have nowhere to fall
But to drown in you

Let the Lady Go

Save your tears-
　　　for a laughter that makes your side pain
　　　and blurs your eyes with uncontainable joy.

Save your tears-
　　　for the moment that your child is born
　　　with a cry of the life that you gave him.

Save your tears-
　　　for your foolishness;
　　　the argument that you deservingly lost,
　　　pulling your pride down to its needed levels.

Save your tears-
　　　for that quiet moment,
　　　when your wife is puttering across the room-
　　　unknowing of your gaze-
　　　and like a forgotten childhood memory
　　　you stop to catch your breath
　　　at the thought of just how much you really love her.

Save your tears-
　　　for the moments of coming home.
　　　The same flowers that bloom year after year,
　　　the smell of old wood,
　　　the familiar creeks of the floor,
　　　and the fleeting moments
　　　when all siblings
　　　are once again under the same roof.

But don't you cry for death.

Don't rest your feet at her door-
　　　no matter how weary you may be.

She is a lady-
　　　who comes and goes
　　　and does her job.

She is a lady,
      so do not gawk.
      Bid her farewell,
      'till she returns
      and gently close the door.
      Then turn to the warm fires of your home
      and tend your children-

You-
      the loved and the living.

Do not weep for death-
      it will not understand
      why you waste your tears
      for the very things
      that have brought you so much life-

You-
      the loved and the living.

Let the lady go.
Come and go,
      and save your tears
      for the things most worthy of them.

Come and go.
Do your job.
Love
      and live.

The Story Of My Inexistence

You're the house I can't come home to
The bed I can't crawl into
You're the bottle that won't get me drunk
And the pain that won't quite kill me
You're the arms I can't wrap around me
You're the soft hair not running through my fingers
You're the comforting voice that's just a memory
You're the beautiful eyes not looking back at mine
You're the warm breath-not on my hair at night
You're the whiskers-not brushing against my cheek
You're the one-not here
You're the voice-not saying, 'I love you'
You're written all over me
You're everywhere I go
You're the one that crowds my heart
You're the loneliness that clings to me
You're the one-not here
You're so much of me
That without you I am inexistent

Grandma's Dream

I drove up to the Grove,
Where they say that time stands still,
And knocked on Grandma's door
To get my wisdom's fill.

We talked of life and death-
Two things most people fear,
Without any sadness,
Without shedding a tear.

She said she'll live to be
A hundred, if not more!
The twinkle in her eye
Told that she knows for sure.

She said there's just too much
That she still wants to see,
"...like man going to Mars.
Oh, what a sight that'd be!"

So on cold winter nights,
She bundles up her head
To gaze up at the stars,
And walk among the dead.

See, the cemetery
Is the best place to view
The sleeping azure sky
From Gramma's avenue.

She stands above the *past*,
Underneath *tomorrow*,
And keeps her mind alive,
Learning from her sorrow.

The light will shine on us

From Cassiopeia.
The brave will sleep below,
Whis'pring, '*Columbia...*'

The odds that man has faced
Are honored with our shroud,
Remembered by our tears,
But done to make us proud.

Every night, the heavens
Will glow on those gone by,
And that sweet old woman,
Who thanks them for their try.

I pray that Grandma's right,
About longevity,
But hope the men at NASA
Fulfill *her* dream for *me*.

In remembrance of the crew of the Columbia shuttle and to my Grandmother's thirst for knowledge and hope for the future.

Denial

I'm not really marching.
I'm not owned by this patch.
We're down at the quarry
Pulling in the catch.

I'm not lying on my stomach,
Squinting through the site.
I'm sitting on your couch,
As the breeze wafts through the night.

I'm not sitting in this class
To the same old boring speech.
We're reminiscing in your kitchen,
Oh, the lessons you did teach.

'Sergeant! Sergeant! What do we do?
Where is this? Where is that?'
When will Dave be home next?
How is Phillip? How is Pat?

I'm not shining the same old boot.
I'm not ironing the same old crease.
Grandma, what did you kill now?
It's good to come home and eat some grease.

I'm not catching a plane.
I'm not really on-the-go.
I'm just driving up the road
To those two familiar steps I know.

My hair's not pulled into a bun.
I'm not communicating by a pen.
No, Grandma, you're not fatter,
But you've combed your curls out again.

I'm not running for my life.
Pull-up? Why not 'pull-down'?
I'm sledding down your hill,
And the girls are goofing around.

I'm not nailing paper targets.
Don't say 4 a.m., I'll cry.
I'm nailing corn out on the tree,
And the squirrels are scurrying by.

*written while I was dreaming of the comfort of Grandma's house while in the Army

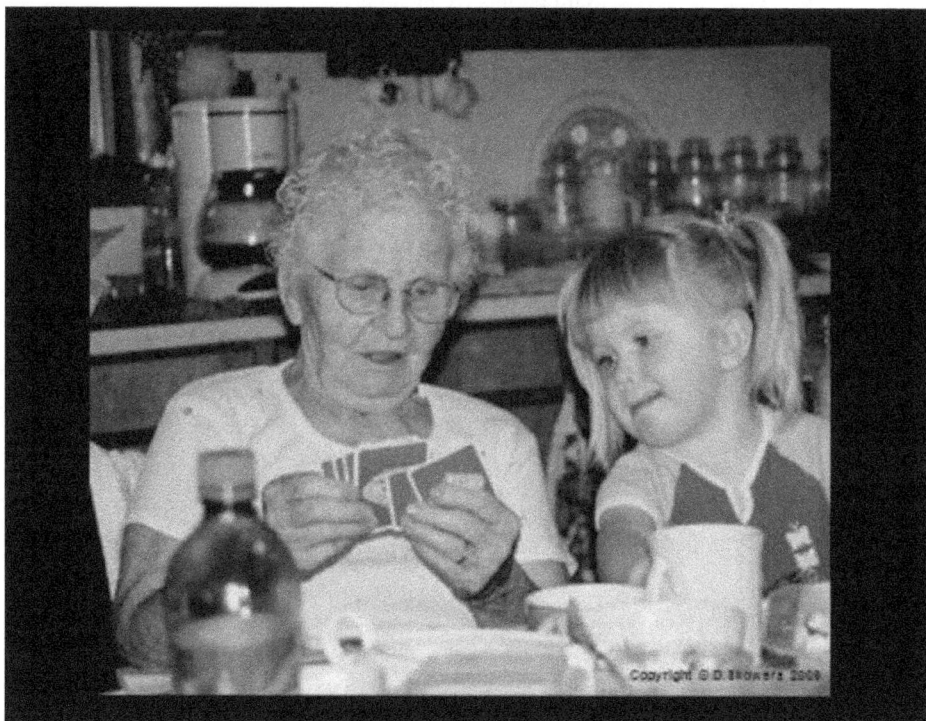

Cadence

*(*sung to *It Won't Be Long)*

I know you wanted me to stay,
But we can't always have our way.
Now you're sitting there at home.
Are you waiting for me all alone?

With bullets flying all around
I keep my head close to the ground.
When the smoke is clear and through-
I keep my thoughts closer to you.

Got your letter in the mail-
Said you miss having me to hold.
Good thing I don't know how to fail,
So soon you'll see me down the road.

Assurances of the Tramp

You won't have to worry,
When I leave this town;
I'll be warm in my shadows,
As long as the sun goes down.

And you won't have to worry
That I'll be chased down;
I've been a piece of meat before,
And know when to stand my ground.

You're silly, if you'll worry
That I won't come back;
This tramp knows where home is,
When to stay, and when to pack.

The Pain is in the Season

The pain is in the season
The love is in the treason
The leaving is just another reason.

The past is in the heart
The future's on the start
Today is just falling apart.

The thought is on the man
The hopes went in the can
I'm just running 'cause I can.

The anger's in the eye
The regret's in the goodbye
I'll just write you when I cry.

Flaws of the Composer

I sat and wrote a sad song;
It flowed so easily,
Until the beat and rhythm
Fit the aching inside me:
The broken-hearted woman,
The sorry love affair,
The couple-not a couple,
Two people-not a pair.
I sank a little lower,
I drowned a little deep,
I stacked chips on my shoulder,
I lost a little sleep.
Another chance been taken.
Another matchbook gone.
Hello-to being shaken.
Hello-to being wrong.
My clothes became a bandage.
My heart-an open sore.
I'm dressing heavy in the sunlight,
And now smiling is a chore.

A Heart Without a Plan

I don't want to leave you,
But I sure can't stay here,
Among the gremlins and the ghouls,
And the walls that hold my fear.

I don't want to leave you,
But I just can't stick around
And be the favored piece
On your playing ground.

I don't want to leave you,
But I never really came;
I thought you'd meet me in the middle,
But I waited in my shame.

I don't want to leave you,
But I'll take what I can-
A pocketful of memories
And a heart without a plan.

Hypocrisy

Quiet as a stone,
I am crowded in alone-
To give all of my recompense
For all of thoughts' irrelevance,
And bound a mirror fore my eyes
To catch the mind's inevitable lies.

I ask,
Who molded the cast?
God created all things.
Then who cast the first *stone*?
Between my eyes and the inevitable
I am crowded-in alone.

The Destination Of Gratitude

Mother-
A sweet word
Of a time when nothing could afflict the soul or heart.

Mother-
A beautiful creature
Capable of all things possible and unconditional love.

Mother-
A comfortable memory,
Always relied upon, when nothing else is going right.

Mother-
The address
Where I send all of my Thank You's.

I Dreamt I Was A Blanket

I dreamt I was a blanket
Of the softest downy fleece
And sleep hit you like drunkenness
Calling you to dreams

You pulled me all around you
And wrapped me up in your soul

I kept you from the chill of the breeze
And coddled you to a slumber
That you had not seen for so long

You basked under my warmth
Protected in sweet repose
I kept you from the cold
I kept you from the piercing light

I kept you safe and warm

I gave you tender dreams
Of carefree days and comfort
You rolled around in me–
Protected

I kept away the sound
I fought for your serenity
I wrapped you up in my soul
And kept you safe and warm

A Girl From the Country

Take your thorns-
You bastard
And don't ever give a rose
To a girl from the country,
With dirt on all her clothes.

Take your sex and money,
And don't ever give 'the time'
To a girl from the country,
Who never had a dime.

Take your words and rhymes
And don't ever give a smile
To a girl from the country,
Who's walked the ragged mile.

Take your warmth and arms
And don't ever give your love
To a girl from the country,
Who's been used like a glove.

Take your beauty and your cheer
And don't ever give a glance
To a girl from the country,
Who never stood a chance.

Where Your Name Fits

I promise not to love you;
  I'll finally set you free,
But confess I keep a corner
  Of my mind for your memory.

That way I won't be faltered,
  When the wolf is at the door,
Or make a mess of things again,
  Just as I have before.

I promise not to love you.
  I'll finally be alone,
Accept for that small corner
  Of my heart you'll always own.

That way I won't be shaken,
  When the wolf is looking in,
For I'll remember all the places
  My heart has already been.

I promise not to love you,
  Not even a little bit-
There's just a place inside me
  Where your name happens to fit.

There

You'll be the man who's always *there*
And *there* will be my heart;
The story of one life,
Consisting of two parts.
And if tears should fall,
Upon your gentle cheek,
Their's will be a pain
That makes me just as weak.
Should distance come between us,
It will only be in miles,
Leaving us to count the hours,
'till we exchange our smiles.

There Was Always Someone

There was always someone
fool enough to believe in me.

I keep my head above the self-pity,
but remind myself enough to remain grateful.

There was always someone
fool enough to believe in me.
They saw through me like a window
and held out a hand I was too proud to take.

So I keep my head high above the self-pity,
and the tears that I don't cry
live in the well of gratitude
deep within me.

Coincidence

When I'm thick in thought
Can you pervade my concentration?
When the fire is near my soul
Will you cool my agitation?

When the road is far before me,
And the journey much too long,
Will my radio breathe glimpses
Of you-in every song?

When my bed feels much too big
And night breezes surround me,
May I roll over and dream-
That your arms are around me?

When gatherings have lost their glow
And laughter only makes me blue,
Is it alright if I pretend
That I'm sitting next to you?

When I'm out and about,
Going from place to place,
Should I blush when I find
I've found a familiar face?

Is it alright you're everywhere
That I happen to be?
If you've gone so far away,
How come you're still here with me?

On Alexander Pope's "Eloisa To Abelard"

There is nothing that I forgot
Of to have and to have not
Or what we are and what we ought

We are suspended in time
A coin in eternal sunshine
Thrown far above the endless brine

Like beggars with and empty plate
We hold no palm out to wait
For the naming of our fate

I look for nothing-there is nothing to find
Everything is as one should mind
I think of you with this spotless mind

My Biggest Fear

My biggest fear

Is that I may sneeze while sitting at home alone one day,

And someone will say, "Bless you."

A note from the author

Thank you for reading the first publication of my poetry collection! I grew up somehow having memorized such poems as *The Charge of the Light Brigade*, *Invictus*, and *An Irish Airman Forsees His Death*. Thus I have long been a fan of the traditional poetic style. Then I realized I would one day exhaust the type of poetry that I so enjoyed because publishers frowned upon rhymed verse and sought more non-traditional verse. Pretty soon the only one left that I knew who shared my love of poetry was my Grandmother. If I had a nickel for every time that she's recited *Daffodils* to me…I'd have a lot of nickels!

I started reading other styles of poetry and found out that anything goes. Some might say otherwise-that there is a method to styles that seem to have little method to me. So I tried my hand at writing unrhymed verse and threw a lot away before I found my own rhythm.

I learned that you really have to have a powerful grasp of description and conveying emotion if you are going to use unrhymed verse and want to leave an impact with the reader. I support any style of poetry as I feel it is an important part of our culture, language, and literature. However, I wanted to show the amplification of emotions, that we don't describe in normal conversation when we talk about our experiences, in my poetry. I wanted to write poems that leave something with people so much that they remember them with ease like their favorite songs. Whether I have done this all depends upon the reader, their style, and the choice of their interpretation.

This has taught me to respect all forms of poetry more than I had in my younger years. Whether you are going to publish your works or not, I'd encourage you to give writing a try. It's an interesting way to recall the change in your outlook, emotions, and personality.

I hope that you enjoy this collection, and I thank you for supporting the arts. Whether we appreciate one person's work over another, I am a strong believer that the literature and poetry we write today will one day reflect historically on our present culture so that generations to come can see what life was like when we were here.

Other works

After Abu Ghraib

By D. Skowera

ISBN 978-1-935444-15-2

The story no one dares to tell…

"After Abu Ghraib" tells of the secretive world of detainee operations. Told by a female interrogator who was part of the first of four interrogation battalions formed in response to the Abu Ghraib abuse scandal. No holding back, this book shows what life was like during Operation Iraqi Freedom for soldiers, civilian contractors, and detainees alike. Learn what life was like "over there" for a unit that made history in a time that will be talked about for ages.

For more information about the author and her works you can visit her website at www.dskowera.com

www.ingramcontent.com/pod-product-compliance
Lightning Source LLC
Chambersburg PA
CBHW021921040426
42448CB00007B/849